GREEK
MYTHS

FIRST EDITION
Series Editor Deborah Lock; **Art Editor** Clare Shedden; **US Editor** John Searcy;
Production Editor Siu Chan; **Production** Erika Pepe; **Picture Researcher** Liz Moore;
Illustrators David Burroughs and Nilesh Mistry; **Reading Consultant** Linda Gambrell, PhD

THIS EDITION
Editorial Management by Oriel Square
Produced for DK by WonderLab Group LLC
Jennifer Emmett, Erica Green, Kate Hale, *Founders*

Editors Grace Hill Smith, Libby Romero, Michaela Weglinski;
Photography Editors Kelley Miller, Annette Kiesow, Nicole DiMella; **Managing Editor** Rachel Houghton;
Designers Project Design Company; **Researcher** Michelle Harris; **Copy Editor** Lori Merritt;
Indexer Connie Binder; **Proofreader** Larry Shea; **Reading Specialist** Dr. Jennifer Albro;
Curriculum Specialist Elaine Larson

Published in the United States by DK Publishing
1745 Broadway, 20th Floor, New York, NY 10019

Copyright © 2023 Dorling Kindersley Limited
DK, a Division of Penguin Random House LLC
23 24 25 26 10 9 8 7 6 5 4 3 2 1
001-333917-June/2023

A catalog record for this book
is available from the Library of Congress.
HC ISBN: 9780-7440-7234-1
PB ISBN: 9780-7440-7235-8

DK books are available at special discounts when purchased in bulk for sales promotions, premiums,
fundraising, or educational use. For details, contact: DK Publishing Special Markets,
1745 Broadway, 20th Floor, New York, NY 10019
SpecialSales@dk.com

Printed and bound in China

The publisher would like to thank the following for their kind permission to reproduce their images:
a=above; c=center; b=below; l=left; r=right; t=top; b/g=background

Alamy Stock Photo: Artokoloro 40bl, Florilegius 12bl, Spencer Grant 28bl, Heritage Image Partnership Ltd /
Historic England Archive 6tl, M.Brodie 9crb, Marcus Roberts Images / Stockimo 30br, SandraC 11tr, Zuri Swimmer 29bc;
Dreamstime.com: Paradoks_blizanaca 31tr; **Getty Images:** De Agostini / DEA / G. DAGLI ORTI 21c, Hulton Archive / Heritage Images /
Contributor 18cl; The J. Paul Getty Museum, Los Angeles: 32cl; **Library of Congress, Washington, D.C.:** LC-USZC4-10060 22tl;
© **The Metropolitan Museum of Art:** Fletcher Fund, 1924 32tl, Gift of Mr. and Mrs. Leon Pomerance, 1953 45tr, Rogers Fund, 1921 7cr,
35cra; **Shutterstock.com:** Adwo 1bc, Dolfilms 25bl, Sergii Figurnyi 10tl

Cover images: *Front:* **Shutterstock.com:** Delcarmat ca, br, rudall30

All other images © Dorling Kindersley
For more information see: www.dkimages.com

For the curious
www.dk.com

Level

4

GREEK
MYTHS

Deborah Lock

CONTENTS

The Written Word
The poets Homer, around 750 BCE, and then Hesiod, in 700 BCE, were the first people to write down Greek myths.

Telling Stories
The first Greek myths were told orally. The stories were passed down from one generation to the next.

Religion
Myths were an important part of the religion in ancient Greece.

STORIES OF OLD

In ancient times, the people of Greece built huge temples where they worshipped their gods and goddesses. Where did the idea of these gods come from? Like all cultures, the Greeks wanted to understand the changing seasons, the weather, why good and bad things happened to them, and what would happen when they died.

Temple of Poseidon

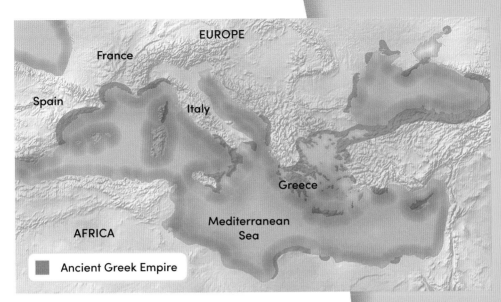

Belief in the Greek gods and goddesses spread throughout the ancient Greek empire.

Their answers lay in the belief that there were gods and goddesses, who took an interest in people's everyday lives. They told stories about these immortals. The stories, which we call myths, included tales of heroes, monsters, and spirits.

Greek Art
Myths were a popular subject in Greek art. Scenes from myths are depicted in ancient Greek sculptures and pottery.

7

Eros
The beautiful son of Aphrodite, Eros [AIR–oss], was the god of love. In myths, he was known for shooting his arrows at people to make them fall in love.

FAMILY OF GREEK GODS

Let's begin at the beginning with the god of the heavens, Uranus [YOUR-uh-nus], and the earth goddess, Gaia. Their children began the race of Titans, a group of powerful giants who roamed the heavens and earth. The youngest, Cronus, the god of time, took control when he killed his father. Aphrodite [af-ro-DIE-tee], the goddess of love, sprang from the sea as Uranus was cut into pieces.

Aphrodite, goddess of love and beauty

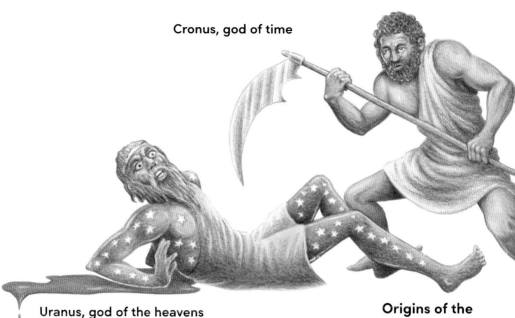

Cronus, god of time

Uranus, god of the heavens

Origins of the Gods
Uranus and Gaia had 12 children: six boys and six girls. These were the first generation of Titans.

Cronus had three sons: Zeus [ZOOS], Poseidon [puh-SIGH-dun], and Hades [HAY-deez]. He also had three daughters: Hestia, Demeter [de-MEE-ter], and Hera [HAIR-a]. It was these immortals and their children who appeared in many of the Greek myths.

Titanic
The word "titanic" comes from the Greek word *titanikos*, which means "big and powerful."

9

Mount Olympus
The peak of Mount Olympus was believed to be the home of the gods.

The Olympians
The 12 gods and goddesses who lived on Mount Olympus were called the Olympians.

Zeus waged a terrifying war against his father and some of the Titans, and he defeated them. He then became the god of heaven and earth and went on to father many gods, goddesses, and heroes. He lived with his wife, Hera, along with Demeter, Aphrodite, and his eight immortal children on Mount Olympus, the highest mountain in Greece.

Zeus, god of the heavens and earth

Hera, goddess of childbirth and marriage

Hestia, the goddess of the hearth and home, gave up her seat on Olympus to look after the fire within the mountain.

Poseidon, the god of the sea, lived in his golden underwater palace, stirring up storms and earthquakes if he was angry.

Poseidon, god of the sea

Hades was the dark god of the underworld—the place where people went when they died.

Hades, god of the underworld

Hestia
In the Greek language, "Hestia" means "hearth." In Greek society, the hearth, or fireplace, was the center of a home.

Poseidon
Poseidon held a three-pronged spear called a trident. It was created by one-eyed giants called the Cyclopes.

Hades
Hades was the name of the god of the underworld and the name of the dark place where he lived.

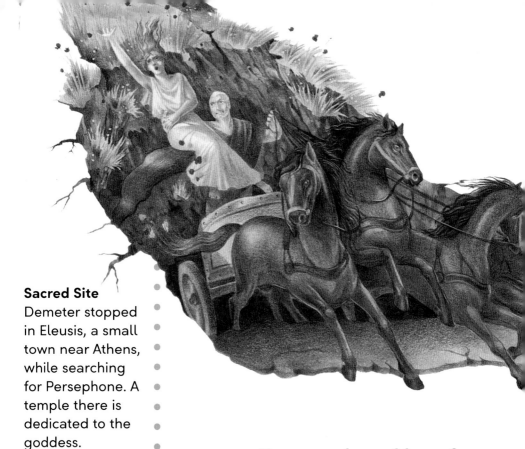

Sacred Site
Demeter stopped in Eleusis, a small town near Athens, while searching for Persephone. A temple there is dedicated to the goddess.

Demeter, the goddess of crops, had a beautiful daughter named Persephone [per-SEFF-uh-nee]. Hades kidnapped Persephone and made her his wife in the underworld. As Demeter grieved, the earth became frozen and nothing grew. Zeus ordered Hades to free Persephone.

Symbols attributed to Demeter include wheat and the Horn of Plenty.

Hades kidnapped Persephone, taking her to the underworld.

When she saw her daughter again, Demeter's sadness melted, winter faded, and the plants grew. However, Persephone had eaten six pomegranate seeds while in the underworld. So, each year she had to spend six months with Hades, and the seasons became fall and winter. She could be with her mother the other six months, and the seasons changed to spring and summer.

Pomegranates
In Greek myths, pomegranates represent life, rebirth, and marriage. By eating a few seeds, Persephone tied herself to Hades.

Splitting Headache
Athena springs from Zeus's head.

Athena's City
Athens, the capital of Greece, was named for Athena after she won a competition against Poseidon.

Many of Zeus's immortal children had unusual birth stories. One day, Zeus had a bad headache. He asked his son Hephaestus [huh-FEST-uss] to split open his head with an axe. Out sprang Athena [a-THEE-na], dressed for battle and shouting her war cry.

Just like us, these titanic Olympians had emotions such as love, jealousy, and anger. They were fascinated by people and meddled in their lives with both heroic and fateful consequences.

Zeus and His Eight Immortal Children

Ares, god of war

Hebe, goddess of youth

Dionysus, god of wine and feasting

Artemis, goddess of the moon and wild animals

Apollo, god of light, music, and healing

Hermes, god of trade, and protector of travelers

Athena, goddess of wisdom and war

Hephaestus, god of the blacksmith's fire

PANDORA'S JAR

According to legend, Zeus wanted to create a race of people. He ordered Prometheus [pro-MEE-thee-us], one of the Titans, to mold men and women out of clay in the likeness of the gods. Zeus then breathed life into the people.

Prometheus
The name "Prometheus" means "forethought." Prometheus was a Titan. He saw that the Titans would only win the war against the Olympians with trickery. The Titans wouldn't listen to him, so he switched sides and helped the Olympians win.

Zeus, god of the heavens and earth

Prometheus lived among the people and taught them how to build homes, grow plants, and hunt animals. He begged Zeus to give them fire so they could cook and make metal tools, but Zeus refused.

"It will make them as powerful as the gods," he said.

However, Prometheus stole some fire from the rising sun. When Zeus saw the people using fire, he was very angry and severely punished Prometheus.

Eternal Punishment
For disobeying Zeus, Prometheus was chained to a high rock and had his liver torn out each day by an eagle. Since he was immortal, his liver grew back every night.

Hephaestus

Hephaestus was the Greek god of fire. He had forges throughout the Greek world, including one in his palace on Mount Olympus. He created weapons, armor, and gifts for the other gods.

Epimetheus

The name "Epimetheus" means "afterthought." While "Prometheus," meaning "forethought," is always a clever character in Greek myths, Epimetheus is always a fool.

Zeus also wanted to punish the people, so he asked Hephaestus to make a woman in his blacksmith's fire. The gods gave her gifts, such as beauty, love, curiosity, and deceit. They named her Pandora meaning "all-gifted."

She was sent to Prometheus's brother, Epimetheus [e-puh-MEE-thee-us]. She was also given a jar, which she was forbidden to open.

Pandora receives the gifts of beauty from Aphrodite, music from Apollo, and deceit from Hermes.

Pandora's Box
Even today, the term "Pandora's box" signifies a source of endless complications and troubles.

Although his brother had warned him not to accept a gift from Zeus, Epimetheus was enchanted with Pandora and married her.

Pandora could not forget about the jar. One day she peeked inside and all the evils flew out into the world—sickness, sin, and death.

As she closed the lid, hope was the only thing left in the jar.

Pandora

LABORS OF HERACLES

This is the tale of the greatest and strongest of all heroes—Heracles [HAIR-uh-kleez]. He was the son of Zeus, but his mother was a mortal woman. Hera was extremely jealous of Heracles. He grew into a determined, wise young man with superhuman strength and skills.

Zeus wanted his son to become a god when he died. Hera replied, "I will only agree to this if Heracles can perform 12 labors to be set forth by his cousin Eurystheus [you-RIS-thee-us], the king of Mycenae [my-SEE-nee]."

Superstrong

As Heracles lay in his cot, Hera sent serpents to kill him. Even though he was only a baby, Heracles strangled the serpents with his bare hands.

Eurystheus hated Heracles and hoped for his death. "Your first task is to kill the lion, which is devouring the people of Nemea," he commanded.

Heracles
Heracles was called Hercules by the Romans. Athena guided Heracles in many of his tasks.

Athena

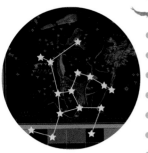

Hercules Constellation

Hercules, based on the Roman adaptation of Heracles, is the fifth-largest constellation in the sky. It is one of the original 48 constellations identified by Ptolemy in the second century. It is visible in the Northern and Southern hemispheres.

The Nemean lion had skin that could not be pierced by weapons. So, Heracles followed the lion to its cave and wrestled with it. After strangling it to death, he returned to Eurystheus, wearing the lion's skin as armor. Heracles successfully completed task after task. His 11th task was to steal some golden apples that grew on a tree in a garden that was guarded by three maidens called the Hesperides [heh-SPARE-uh-deez], along with a fierce serpent.

After seeking advice from the gods, Heracles went first to the Hesperides' father, Atlas. Atlas was one of the Titans defeated long ago by Zeus. His everlasting punishment was to hold up the heavens on his shoulders. "If you ask your daughters for a couple of apples," offered Heracles, "I'll hold up the heavens for a while."

Herculean Tasks
Heracles' tasks included killing or capturing many of the fiercest mythical animals.

Atlas
The name "Atlas" in Greek can mean "suffering" or "very enduring."

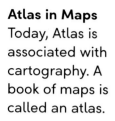

Atlas in Maps
Today, Atlas is associated with cartography. A book of maps is called an atlas.

Atlas agreed but asked Heracles to kill the serpent first. Heracles did this by shooting a single arrow over the garden wall. He then took up Atlas's burden. When Atlas returned with the apples, he did not want to take the heavens back.

"I'd be delighted to continue," said Heracles, "but could you just take them for a moment so that I can make a grassy cushion for my shoulder?"

When Atlas took the heavens back, Heracles picked up the apples and walked away. He then went on to complete his 12th labor. Zeus was pleased. When Heracles died, he joined the gods on Mount Olympus. He became the guardian of the door to the heavens.

Atlas in Art
Atlas is forever holding up the world on his shoulders in paintings, sculptures, and other works of art.

The Final Challenge
Heracles' 12th labor was to go to the underworld and bring back Hades' three-headed dog, Cerberus.

Greece

Crete

Legacy
The Minoan civilization, which existed on Crete, was named after King Minos.

King Minos
King Minos was one of the most famous kings in Greek mythology. He was a son of Zeus.

THESEUS AND THE MINOTAUR

Just off the coast of Greece is an island called Crete. It was here, say the myths, that a most fearsome creature called the Minotaur lived during the reign of King Minos. The Mintoaur was half-man and half-bull and ate only human flesh. The beast was so terrible that the king commanded his greatest craftsman, Daedalus [DED-uh-lus], to build a labyrinth that no one could escape from. At the center of this maze lived the Minotaur.

Every nine years, seven boys and seven girls were sent from Athens to be fed to the Minotaur. This was payment from the King of Athens, Aegeus [uh-GEE-us], for accidentally causing the death of Minos's son many years before. The third payment was now due.

Bulls of Knossos
When the ancient palace of Knossos in Crete was excavated, images of bulls were found. Some think this proves that the ancient Cretans worshipped bulls.

Maritime Messages
Colors and symbols on ship sails are commonly used to send messages. A white flag with a red X, for example, means "I need help!"

In Athens, the victims were being selected. A young prince named Theseus offered to go and kill the Minotaur. He was the adopted son of Aegeus and the son of the sea-god Poseidon.

The ship that Theseus took to Crete had black sails, but this time the crew took white sails with them.

"If you succeed, raise the white sails on your return," said Aegeus to his son.

When they arrived at Crete, the Athenians were met by King Minos and his daughter, Ariadne. She fell in love with Theseus at first sight.

"I'll help you kill the Minotaur if you take me back to Athens and make me your wife," Ariadne said to Theseus. He agreed.

Poseidon,
god of the sea

Ariadne
and Theseus

Theseus
Theseus volunteered to face the Minotaur so no more children of Athens would be eaten.

Word Origins
The word "Minotaur" comes from the Greek words for "Minos" and "bull." "Minotaur" is a compound word that means "bull of Minos."

"Tie one end of this magical ball of thread to the entrance of the labyrinth and follow it to the center," Ariadne instructed. "Go at night while the Minotaur sleeps. After killing it, roll the thread back up and it will lead you out."

That night, the glimmering thread led Theseus to the Minotaur, which he wrestled and killed. When he arrived back at the entrance, Ariadne and the Athenians were waiting. They boarded their ship and set sail for Athens.

The Minotaur
The Minotaur's actual name in Greek mythology was Asterion. In ancient Greek, this word means "starry one." The Minotaur is associated with the constellation Taurus, a bull.

On the way, Theseus left Ariadne asleep on the island of Naxos because he did not love her. He also forgot to change the sails from black to white. When King Aegeus saw the black sails, he thought his son was dead and threw himself into the sea. Theseus's triumphant return was overshadowed by grief.

King Aegeus
The body of water where King Aegeus died is now known as the Aegean Sea.

THE FALL OF ICARUS

King Minos was furious that Theseus had succeeded in defeating the Minotaur. He put the inventor of the labyrinth, Daedalus, and his lazy son, Icarus, into prison. Daedalus started planning how to escape.

He collected feathers from passing birds and made two pairs of wings by threading the feathers together and sealing them with wax from their candles. Finally, they were ready to escape.

Daedalus
An early type of Greek art was named after Daedalus. It is called Daedalic sculpture.

"Put on these wings,"
Daedalus told Icarus.
"Follow me, and don't fly
too high or too low."

They both took flight over the
sea. Icarus was careful at first, but
then soared upward, feeling free
like a bird. The sun's heat then
melted his wings and he tumbled
to his death.

When Daedalus looked back for
his son, he could see only feathers
floating on the water.

Icarus
The part of the
Aegean Sea
where Icarus is
said to have
fallen is now
known as the
Icarian Sea. The
island where his
body washed
ashore was
named Ikaría.

Perseus

Perseus was the first Greek hero. In Greek myths, he lived several generations before Heracles was born.

THE ADVENTURES OF PERSEUS

There was a young man named Perseus, who lived with his beautiful mother, Danae [DAN-ay-ee], on the island of Seriphos [SEH-ri-fos]. The evil king, Polydectes, wanted to marry Danae, but Perseus protected her.

So, Polydectes tricked Perseus into attempting an impossible task. Polydectes held a feast. Being poor, Perseus came with no gift, but he promised the king a present.

"Bring me the head of the Gorgon Medusa," challenged Polydectes.

The Gorgons were three fearsome, scaly monsters, who had snakes for hair. Anyone who looked at Medusa's face turned to stone.

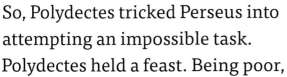

Medusa
The Gorgons were sisters. Unlike her sisters, Medusa was mortal and could be killed.

Nymphs

Nymphs were female spirits who protected natural things such as mountains, valleys, rivers, trees, wind, and rain.

Sickle

A sickle is a long, curved, metal blade with a short handle. It is a tool used in agriculture to cut tall grass or grain.

Perseus's father was none other than Zeus. From Olympus, Zeus sent Athena and Hermes to help his son. They gave him the shiniest shield and the sharpest sickle in the world.

Following their advice, Perseus then visited the nymphs of the North Wind. These female spirits loaned him some winged sandals, a leather bag, and Hades' Cap of Invisibility.

Wearing the sandals and cap, Perseus flew unseen to the far west where he found the three Gorgons asleep. Looking only at Medusa's reflection in the shield, he cut off her head with the sickle and put it into the bag.

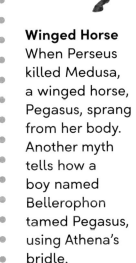

Winged Horse
When Perseus killed Medusa, a winged horse, Pegasus, sprang from her body. Another myth tells how a boy named Bellerophon tamed Pegasus, using Athena's bridle.

The beheading of Medusa

Andromeda's Situation
Poseidon, god of the sea, was angry at Andromeda's mother. She had been bragging that Andromeda was more beautiful than the Nereid sea nymphs. The Nereids were admired for their outstanding beauty.

As Perseus flew home, he saw a beautiful princess, Andromeda [an-DRAH-muh-duh], chained to a rock. Her parents had angered Poseidon and were sacrificing her to a sea monster to appease him.

As the monster rose from the waves, Perseus held up Medusa's head and turned it to stone.

Perseus married Andromeda and took her back to Seriphos.

King Polydectes had made Danae a slave and was surprised to see Perseus.

"Where's my gift?" he asked.

Without a word, Perseus held up the head of Medusa and turned the king to stone.

Story in the Stars
Several well-known star patterns have been named after the characters in Perseus's story. These include Perseus, Andromeda, her parents, and the sea monster.

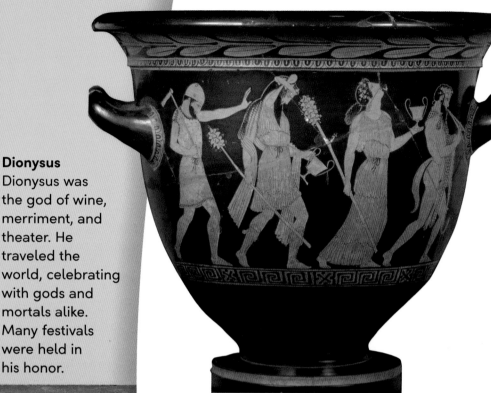

Dionysus
Dionysus was the god of wine, merriment, and theater. He traveled the world, celebrating with gods and mortals alike. Many festivals were held in his honor.

THE FOOLISHNESS OF MIDAS

Not all myths are about heroes. Some tell of very foolish mortals who misused gifts from the gods. One such person was King Midas.

One day, Midas found an old satyr named Silenus in his garden. Silenus was drunk after feasting with the god Dionysus.

King Midas looked after Silenus very well and then returned him to Dionysus, who lived by the banks of the River Pactolus. In thanks, Dionysus promised Midas any gift he wanted.

"Let everything I touch turn to gold," replied Midas, greedily.

His wish was granted.

Dionysus

Midas

Mischievous Satyrs
Satyrs were roguish male spirits of nature who roamed the woods and mountains. They were half-man and half-goat and had horns, hooves, and tails.

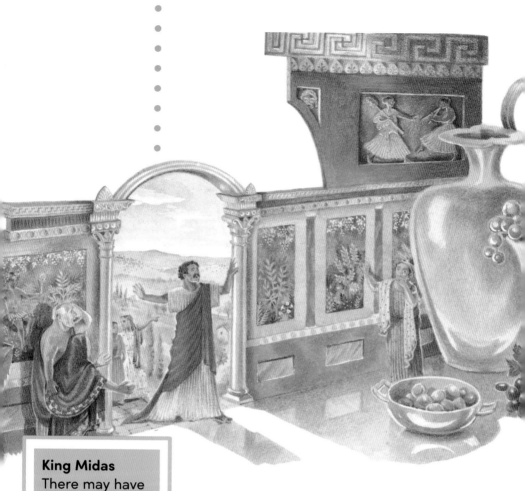

King Midas
There may have been a real King Midas. In the eighth century BCE, King Mita ruled the kingdom of Phrygia, which is in modern-day Turkey. His kingdom was known for its gold and wealth.

With delight, Midas turned his palace and all the trees and flowers in his garden to gold.

However, his pleasure was short-lived. As he picked up food and drank his wine, they also turned to gold. Then, he hugged his daughter. To his horror, she turned to gold, too.

Midas returned to Dionysus and begged to be freed from his gift.

"Wash away your greed in the spring of the River Pactolus," Dionysus told him.

As Midas bathed in the river, the water turned to gold.

Still, Midas had not learned from his foolishness.

The Midas Touch
The term "Midas touch" is still used today to describe someone who succeeds at everything they try.

43

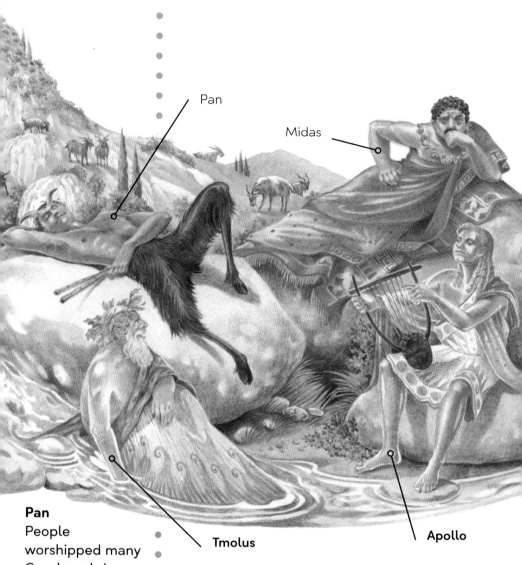

Pan

Midas

Tmolus

Apollo

Pan
People worshipped many Greek gods in temples. Because Pan was the god of nature, they worshipped him in caves.

Midas was a worshipper of Pan, the mischievous goat-like god of wild places. He enjoyed listening to Pan play country tunes on his reed pipes.

One day, Pan boasted that he was a better musician than Apollo, the god of music, and challenged him to a contest.

The contest was to be judged by the river god Tmolus [MO-lus]. Midas came along to listen and judge for himself.

Pan's merry tunes were no match for Apollo's lilting lyre music, and Tmolus awarded the prize to Apollo. However, Midas said he preferred Pan's playing. In anger, Apollo gave Midas a pair of long, hairy donkey ears. Midas covered his ears in a turban, but people found out about them and he died of shame.

Lyre
A lyre is a U-shaped harp. In ancient Greece, singers and poets were often accompanied by lyre music when they performed.

GLOSSARY

Excavate
To dig up something of historical interest

God
A male immortal with power over nature and human affairs, who is believed in and worshipped by people

Goddess
A female immortal with power over nature and human affairs, who is believed in and worshipped by people

Gorgons
Three frightening female creatures with snakes for hair and golden wings

Hero
A mortal who is known for doing great deeds

Immortal
A supernatural being that lives forever

Labor
A task that requires great effort

Labyrinth
A difficult maze big enough for people to walk through

Mortal
A person who will die someday

Mount Olympus
The highest mountain in Greece. The ancient Greeks believed their gods and goddesses lived on the peak.

Myth
A traditional story about supernatural beings and heroes

Nymphs
Minor goddesses of nature written about in myths

Pegasus
A winged horse that sprang from the body of Medusa

Pomegranate
A hard, red fruit about the size of an orange, containing many large seeds within a juicy, red pulp

Satyr
A half-human, half-animal woodland god

Superhuman
Having greater abilities than a normal person

Temple
A place where gods and goddesses are worshipped

Titans
A family of giants featured in Greek myths

Underworld
The place where ancient Greeks believed they would go when they died

INDEX

QUIZ

Answer the questions to see what you have learned. Check your answers in the key below.

1. Which Greek god led the fight against the Titans?

2. Why are the Greek gods called Olympians?

3. How did Pandora come to be?

4. How many labors did Heracles have to complete?

5. What was Theseus's great accomplishment?

6. Why did Icarus fall from the sky?

7. What kind of creature was Medusa?

8. Which Greek god gave King Midas the golden touch?

1. Zeus 2. They live on Mount Olympus 3. Prometheus made her in his blacksmith's fire 4. 12 5. He killed the Minotaur 6. He flew too close to the sun and his wax wings melted 7. A Gorgon 8. Dionysus